KU-244-314

What if your home was melting away?

Polar Bear

the
BIG
PICTURE

Angela Royston

Published 2010 by
A&C Black Publishers Ltd.
36 Soho Square, London, W1D 3QY

www.acblack.com

ISBN HB 978-1-4081-2794-0
      PB 978-1-4081-3155-8

DUDLEY PUBLIC LIBRARIES

L

748470   SCH

J599.744

Text copyright © 2010 Angela Royston

The right of Angela Royston to be identified as the author of this work has been asserted by her in accordance with the Copyrights, Designs and Patents Act 1988.

A CIP catalogue for this book is available from the British Library.

All rights reserved. No part of this publication may be reproduced in any form or by any means – graphic, electronic or mechanical, including photocopying, recording, taping or information storage and retrieval systems – without the prior permission in writing of the publishers.

Every effort has been made to trace copyright holders and to obtain their permission for use of copyright material. The author and publishers would be pleased to rectify any error or omission in future editions.

This book is produced using paper that is made from wood grown in managed, sustainable forests. It is natural, renewable and recyclable. The logging and manufacturing processes conform to the environmental regulations of the country of origin.

Produced for A&C Black by Calcium. www.calciumcreative.co.uk

Printed and bound in China by C&C Offset Printing Co.

All the internet addresses given in this book were correct at the time of going to press. The author and publishers regret any inconvenience caused if addresses have changed or sites have ceased to exist, but can accept no responsibility for any such changes.

Acknowledgements

The publishers would like to thank the following for their kind permission to reproduce their photographs:

Cover: Shutterstock: Jan Martin Will (front); DigitalVision: Joel Simon (back). **Pages:** DigitalVision: Joel Simon 1, 14, 20; Fotolia: Alexander 12-13, Outdoorsman 16; Istockphoto: Erlend Kvalsvik 10-11, John Pitcher 16-17; Shutterstock: Henrik Winther Andersen 3, 18-19, Antoine Beyeler 8-9, FloridaStock 4, 24, Gentoo Multimedia Ltd. 4-5 (background), Andreas Gradin 13, Käfer photo 7, Keith Levit 20-21, Lena Lir 15, Tyler Olson 14-15, Bernd Schmidt 6, Sergey Smolin 5, Robert St-Coeur 11, TTphoto 6-7 (background), VikOl 9, Yui 22-23, Zingarello 19.

Contents

Polar Home

Polar bears live in the Arctic. **It is very cold here all year round.**

Ice is nice!

Polar bears never feel cold. They have two layers of fur and a thick layer of fat under their skin to keep them warm.

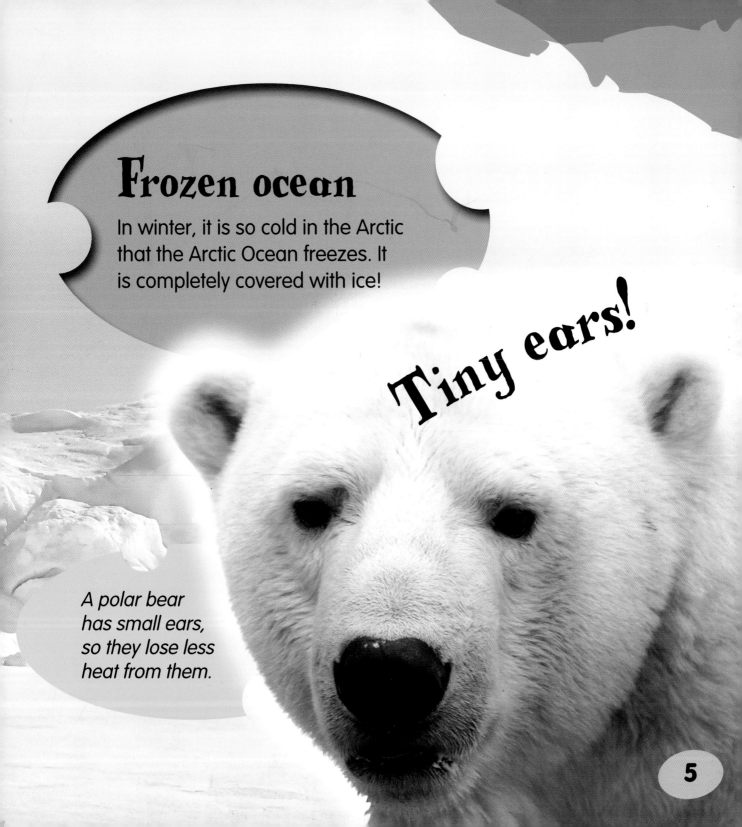

Frozen ocean

In winter, it is so cold in the Arctic that the Arctic Ocean freezes. It is completely covered with ice!

Tiny ears!

A polar bear has small ears, so they lose less heat from them.

Bear Bodies

Polar bears are the biggest meat-eaters on Earth. They are twice as big as a tiger!

Lots of teeth

Polar bears have 42 super-sharp teeth. They use them for slicing up the meat that they eat.

Open wide

Paddle paws

Polar bears have stretchy skin between their claws. This makes their paws a little like a duck's webbed feet. Polar bears use their paws as paddles when they swim.

Polar bears are covered in lots of white fur.

Dinner Time

Polar bears mainly eat meat. Seals are polar bears' favourite food.

Up for air

Seals live underwater, but they breathe air. In winter, they make holes in the sea ice to reach the air above.

There's one!

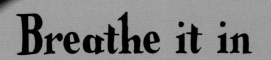

Breathe it in

Seals and polar bears are both **mammals**. Mammals cannot breathe in water, like fishes do. They have to breathe in air.

Polar bears wait by ice holes for seals to come up for air.

Let's Hunt

The best time for polar bears to hunt is spring, while the sea ice still covers the ocean.

Melting ice

After spring, the weather gets warmer and the sea ice begins to melt. The ice breaks up into chunks called ice floes.

Keep up!

Can't catch me!

As the ice melts, the seals no longer need to make breathing holes. This makes it much harder for the polar bears to catch seals.

A seal can easily swim away from a polar bear.

Hungry Bears

In summer, there is less sea ice and fewer seals than at any other time of the year.

Drifting away

Some hungry polar bears stay on the sea ice as it melts. These bears can drift far from land.

I'm stuck!

Polar snacks

In summer, polar bears
eat whatever they can.
They snack on birds
and birds' eggs, and
they even eat **seaweed**.

*Hungry polar bears
sometimes catch
reindeer to eat.*

13

Winter Wait

It gets colder in autumn. Polar bears wait for the sea ice to freeze – then they can hunt for seals again.

Late freeze

Global warming means that the ice is freezing later than it used to, which means the bears have even less time to hunt.

Watch out!

Polar bears are very hungry by the autumn. They are fiercer and more dangerous now than at any other time.

Grrrrr!

A hungry polar bear will eat almost anything!

Baby Bears

Now it is winter. A mother polar bear gives birth to cubs **in November or December.**

Looking after babies

When the cubs are born, the mother bear feeds them with her milk. She does not leave the cubs, even to hunt.

When they are older, the mother teaches her cubs to hunt.

Hungry mums

Before her cubs are born, the mother must eat lots of seals to put on enough fat to keep her going through the winter.

Stay close!

17

In Trouble

The Arctic is becoming warmer. Sea ice is melting earlier in spring, which means polar bears have less time to hunt.

Too far to swim

Some polar bears try to swim far from land to the sea ice to hunt for more seals.

Whooosh!

Getting warmer

The whole Earth is becoming warmer. This is called global warming. Global warming is making the Arctic warmer, too. This is why the ice is melting.

If a bear swims too far from land, it may drown.

Help Us

Polar bears need your help. If we can slow down global warming, the sea ice in the Arctic will stop melting so quickly.

Save the bears

Polar bears have lived on Earth for thousands of years. But if we don't stop global warming, they may soon be gone forever.

Stop global warming and save the polar bear.

Stop the melt!

Here are a few ways you can help:
* Turn off lights to save electricity.
* Take a shower instead of a bath.
* Cycle to school. Don't go by car.

Do it for us

Glossary

Arctic land and seas that surround the North Pole, part of the world that is furthest north

cubs baby animals, such as bear or tiger cubs

global warming the warming up of Earth's surface. Burning fossil fuels such as coal and oil causes global warming.

mammals all animals that have fur or hair. Mammal mothers feed their babies with milk which they make in their bodies.

reindeer a large mammal with antlers that lives on the lands around the Arctic Ocean

seaweed plants that grow in the sea

Further Reading

Websites

Find out what you can do to help polar bears at:
www.polarbearsinternational.org

Discover more about polar bears at:
www.kidzone.ws/sg/polarbear/polar_bear.htm

The National Geographic site has lots of information about polar bears. Find it at:
kids.nationalgeographic.com/Animals/ CreatureFeature/Polar-bear

Books

Face to Face with Polar Bears by Norbert Rosing & Elizabeth Carney, National Geographic (2007).

Global Warming (Protect Our Planet) by Angela Royston, Heinemann Library (2008).

Polar Bears (A True Book) by Ann O. Squire, Children's Press (2007).

Index